World in Focus
Mexico

HODDER
Wayland

CELIA TIDMARSH

First published in 2006 by Hodder Wayland,
an imprint of Hodder Children's Books

© Hodder Wayland 2006

Commissioning editor: Victoria Brooker
Editor: Kelly Davis
Inside design: Chris Halls, www.mindseyedesign.co.uk
Cover design: Hodder Wayland

 Series concept and project management by EASI-Educational Resourcing
(info@easi-er.co.uk)
Statistical research: Anna Bowden
Maps and graphs: Martin Darlison, Encompass Graphics

British Library Cataloguing in Publication Data
Tidmarsh, Celia
   Mexico. - (World in focus)
   1. Mexico - Juvenile literature
   I. Title
   972'0841

ISBN: 0750246820

Printed and bound in China

Hodder Children's Books
A division of Hodder Headline Limited
338 Euston Road, London NW1 3BH

Cover top: Young Mexicans enjoy a country with increasing regional and global influence,
but social divides and economic inequalities are still a problem.
Cover bottom: Mayan site in Yucatán.
Title page: Secondary students in Los Mochis.

Picture acknowledgements
The author and publisher would like to thank the following for allowing their pictures
to be reproduced in this publication:
Corbis 9 (Gianni Dagli Orti), 28 (Keith Dannemiller); EASI-Images/Edward Parker cover top,
4, cover bottom and 5, 6, 8, 10, 11, 12, 13, 14, 15, 16, 17, 18, 19, 20, 21, 22, 23, 24, 25, 26, 27, 29, 30,
31, 32, 33, 34, 35, 36, 37, 38, 39, 40, 41, 42, 43 and title page, 44, 45, 46, 47, 48, 49(t), 49(b), 50, 51, 52,
53, 54, 56, 57, 58 and 59.

The website addresses (URLs) included in this book were valid at the time of
going to press. However, because of the nature of the Internet, it is possible that
some addresses may have changed, or sites may have changed or closed down
since publication. While the author and Publishers regret any inconvenience this
may cause the readers, no responsibility for any such changes can be accepted
by either the author or the Publisher.

The directional arrow portrayed on the map on page 7 provides only an
approximation of north. The data used to produce the graphics and data
panels in this title were the latest available at the time of production.

CONTENTS

CHAPTER 1

Mexico – An Overview

Mexico is part of North America, and it is located between the wealthy, economically developed United States to the north and the less economically developed countries of Central and South America to the south. It is part of a region known as Latin America, which is made up of the countries in Central and South America and the Caribbean that have Spanish or Portuguese as their main language.

The World Bank describes Mexico as a middle-income country that is more prosperous than most of Latin America, but less wealthy than the United States. In 2003, the average Mexican's income (before tax) was US$6,230, compared to US$37,610 in the USA and US$2,710 in Brazil. However, the average figure hides extremes of wealth and poverty. Mexico has one of the most unequal societies in the world.

▼ The second-largest city in the world, Mexico City is sprawling, polluted and overcrowded. It is the centre of government and commerce in Mexico.

MEXICO'S PEOPLE AND HISTORY

The people of Mexico include different cultural groups, with the majority being *mestizo* (mixed race). The population growth rate used to be very high, and approximately 50 per cent of the population today is under 25. However, growth has slowed in recent years, dropping from 2 per cent a year during the 1990s to 1.5 per cent in 2000, and improvements in healthcare have extended average life expectancy to 75 today (compared to only 66 in 1980). Three-quarters of the population live in urban areas. Mexico City, the capital of Mexico, has the second-largest urban population in the world, with an estimated 19 million people in 2005.

Mexico has a fascinating history, including the ancient Aztec and Mayan civilizations, colonization by Spain, and a revolution to get rid of a dictator. Mexico's struggle to become an independent, democratic nation has featured charismatic leaders and much bloodshed. The country's dramatic past has helped to shape Mexican national identity. Mexican culture is very rich, including ancient rituals, numerous festivals, and a cuisine that combines influences from the distant past and from Spain.

 Did you know?

At 2,240 m (7,350 feet) above sea level, Mexico City is the fourth-highest city in the world, after La Paz in Bolivia, Quito in Ecuador, and Bogotá in Colombia.

▼ Tulum, in Yucatán, is a Mayan site dating from about AD 900. Overlooking the Caribbean, the site was probably a fortress protecting a sea port, with the main temple visible from the sea.

MOUNTAINS AND MINERALS

Mexico's landscapes are very varied, ranging from arid deserts to lush rainforests. Mountains cover about 75 per cent of the land area. Mexico is one of the most biodiverse countries on Earth, with over 26,000 plant species, almost 500 different mammals and over 1,000 types of birds. Located on an active section of the Earth's crust, Mexico experiences occasional seismic events such as earthquakes and volcanic eruptions. Volcanic activity in the past has given rise to mineral deposits that are widely distributed across the country. At least 60 minerals were first discovered in Mexico, including silver and copper.

▼ Pico de Orizaba, in Veracruz, is Mexico's highest mountain at 5,700 m (18,700 feet). A dormant volcano, it last erupted in 1546. The Aztecs called it Citlatépetl, meaning 'Star Mountain', because moonlight reflects off its snowy peak.

ECONOMIC AND ENVIRONMENTAL CHALLENGES

There are a number of challenges that Mexico has to face in the present day and into the future. One of these is to match economic development with the growing numbers of people who need jobs. Many Mexican workers migrate to the United States to find work, and some of them do so illegally, which has caused problems between the governments of Mexico and the USA. Since the 1994 North American Free Trade Agreement (NAFTA), there has been an increase in the factories that manufacture goods for sale in the USA, known as *maquiladoras*, built just south of the border into Mexico. These provide the largely unskilled jobs that many Mexicans need. However, they often produce hazardous waste, which causes serious environmental problems. Future economic development will need to be carried out in ways that do not harm the environment. In the past, industrialization in Mexico has caused a great deal of environmental damage. The Mexican government now recognizes that there is an urgent need to repair this damage and to ensure that conservation is given high priority.

Physical geography

- ☐ Land area: 1,923,040 sq km/742,486 sq miles
- ☐ Water area: 49,510 sq km/19,116 sq miles
- ☐ Total area: 1,972,550 sq km/761,602 sq miles
- ☐ World rank (by area): 15
- ☐ Land boundaries: 4,353 km/2,703 miles
- ☐ Border countries: Belize, Guatemala, USA
- ☐ Coastline: 9,330 km/5,794 miles
- ☐ Highest point: Pico de Orizaba (5,700 m/18,700 feet)
- ☐ Lowest point: Laguna Salada (-10 m/-33 ft)

Source: CIA World Factbook

UNITED STATES OF AMERICA

Tijuana 116°
Mexicali 112°
Ensenada
32°
32°
108°
Ciudad Juárez
104°
♦ Casa Grande
Ojinaga
Hermosillo Chihuahua
Obregón
Los Mochis
Torreón
Saltillo
Chupaderos
Durango
La Paz
Tropic of Cancer
Culiacán
Mazatlán
112°
108°
San Luis Potosí
Aguascalientes
Tepic
León
Guadalajara
Tlaquepaque
Colima
Morelia
Querétaro
Teotihuacán
Toluca
Cuernavaca
Popocatépetl 5,465m
Guanajuato
20°
Yaqui
SIERRA MADRE OCCIDENTAL
COPPER CANYON
COHUILA
Rio Grande
Conchos
MEXICO
100°
28°
Nuevo Laredo
Monterrey
Reynosa
Matamoros
SIERRA MADRE ORIENTAL
Ciudad Victoria
24°
Tampico
96°
Bay of Campeche
Poza Rica
MÉXICO CITY
Veracruz
Pico de Orizaba 5,700m
Puebla Orizaba
MICHOACAN
SIERRA MADRE DEL SUR
Acapulco
100° 16°
Oaxaca
Villahermosa
Tuxtla Gutiérrez
92°
88°
Gulf of California
BAJA CALIFORNIA
24°
28°
116°

Gulf of Mexico

92°
Campeche
Mérida Cancún
YUCATÁN PENINSULA
QUINTANA ROO
20°
88°
BELIZE
16°
Caribbean Sea

PACIFIC OCEAN

104°

Gulf of Tehuantepec
96°
GUATEMALA HONDURAS
COSTA RICA

N

Legend
★ Capital
● Cities > 1,000,000
● Cities > 500,000
• Other towns
▲ Mountain
⏣ Volcano
♦ Ancient site

0   200   400 kilometres
0   200   400 miles

CHAPTER 2

History

Ancient Mexico was part of a region called Mesoamerica. Bigger than present-day Mexico, it included areas to the north that today make up Texas, New Mexico, Arizona and California, and to the south, land which is now Belize, Guatemala, El Salvador, Honduras and Nicaragua.

▼ This massive pyramid, rising to over 60 m (197 feet) and among the biggest in the world, dominates the archaeological site of Teotihuacán. It was one of the most impressive cities of the ancient world, covering an area of 20 sq km (8 sq miles).

FROM NOMADS TO CIVILIZATIONS

Between around 1500 BC and AD 1300, many civilizations lived in the area that eventually became modern-day Mexico. The first of these were the Olmecs. Around 500 BC, as the Olmecs died out, other civilizations were growing. From about 200 BC to AD 900, many cities were established, including Teotihuacán (near present-day Mexico City). Between AD 400 and 500, Teotihuacán was the sixth-largest city in the world, with a population of over 150,000. However, during the seventh century, the city outgrew its water and food resources, and declined. Another important civilization at this time was the Mayas. The Mayas are thought to have lived in an area encompassing El Salvador, Guatemala and southern Mexico. They built cities and religious sites, and had sophisticated systems of mathematics,

▲ The Mayas, and the Aztecs, shown here, grew crops on *chinampas* (raised floating beds, made from reeds, mud and manure).

astronomy and writing. In mathematics, for example, they used a base 20 counting system. And in astronomy, they observed and predicted solar and lunar eclipses.

The last great Mesoamerican civilization was the Aztecs. They had a well-developed system of agriculture and an efficient military force. Led by their ruler, Tlacaelel, they expanded their territory and by the late 1400s they were the most powerful people in the area that is present-day Mexico.

THE SPANISH CONQUEST

In 1519, Hernán Cortés, a Spanish explorer, led Spanish troops, known as *Los Conquistadores* (meaning 'The Conquerors'), to Mexico in search of gold and silver. They landed at Veracruz and headed for Tenochtitlán.

Focus on: The Aztecs

The Aztecs originally migrated from the north into central Mexico. They believed that one of their gods, Huitzilopochtli, had prophesied that they would settle where an eagle was seen, sitting on a cactus, eating a snake. The eagle was apparently sighted on an island in Lake Texcoco and the city of Tenochtitlán was founded (now the site of Mexico City). Tenochtitlán flourished, and the Aztecs fought many wars to gain territory and to capture people for sacrifice to their gods who, they believed, needed human hearts in return for good harvests.

The king of the Aztecs, Moctezuma II, at first thought that Cortés was the great god Huitzilopochtli returning, and greeted him warmly. However, the Spanish murdered the Aztec king and took over Tenochtitlán. By 1521, the Aztecs had been defeated and Mexico had been renamed New Spain. Three centuries of Spanish colonial rule followed, and Spain amassed great wealth from Mexico's resources including its rich silver deposits. In New Spain, wealthy Spanish colonists ruled over the powerless indigenous population.

THE FIGHT FOR INDEPENDENCE AND BEYOND

Poor peasants in the rural areas deeply resented the inequalities of colonial society. The fight for independence from Spain began in 1810, led by Miguel Hidalgo, a priest. Hidalgo was executed but the unrest continued. After many uprisings and approximately 600,000 deaths, Mexico finally won its independence in 1821. On 16 September every year, Mexicans still celebrate the day when Hidalgo called them to rise up and fight for their freedom.

The decades from the 1820s to the 1850s saw a great many changes of government. General Antonio Lopez de Santa Ana took over the presidency eleven times between 1823 and 1855. Under his leadership, Mexico lost nearly half its territory to the USA in a war that lasted from 1846 to 1848. Santa Ana was overthrown soon after this. Civil war and an invasion by the French followed, before another army officer, Porfirio Diaz, became president in 1876. He ruled as a ruthless and efficient dictator for 34 years.

◀ The Angel of Independence monument, erected in Mexico City in 1910, commemorates those who fought against Spanish colonial rule.

THE MEXICAN REVOLUTION

The Mexican Revolution began in 1910 when Porfirio Diaz declared himself president again and forced his opponent, Francisco Madero, to flee to Texas. Opposition to Diaz was widespread. The middle classes wanted more political power, most peasants had no land, and living conditions in urban areas were terrible. For instance, in Mexico City health, water and sanitation facilities were so poor that average life expectancy was only 24 years. Peasants' and workers' uprisings, led by Emiliano Zapata, Venustiano Carranza and Pancho Villa, forced Diaz to resign in 1911.

Francisco Madero then became president but the unrest continued and he too resigned. He was replaced by the ruthless and unpopular General Victoriano Huerta. Once again, the revolutionary leaders Zapata, Carranza and Villa joined forces to get Huerta to stand down. After two more years of fighting, and the withdrawal of US government support for Huerta, the

▲ On Independence Day, there are fiestas and parades throughout Mexico, with fireworks, music and children dressing in national costume.

Focus on: Porfirio Diaz

In 1910, after a military coup, Porfirio Diaz proclaimed himself president. He introduced a programme of modernization and the Mexican economy thrived, but he used his brutal police force to suppress any opposition to his rule. He also gave land to his trusted supporters, while most Mexicans remained poor and landless.

 Did you know?

In 1521, the indigenous population was estimated at 20 million. By the mid-seventeenth century, this had dropped to 1 million. The main reason for this high death rate was diseases, such as smallpox and measles, which were brought into Mexico by Europeans.

revolutionaries succeeded and Huerta fled. The revolutionaries then had to rule the country but could not agree which of them should be in charge. Zapata and Villa together opposed Carranza and marched into Mexico City to take over the National Palace. However, both Zapata, who came from the southern state of Morelos, and Villa, from Chihuahua in the north, were more concerned with their home regions and soon returned to them.

Carranza's army defeated Villa's forces, and Carranza became president in 1917, establishing the constitution that is still in place today.

However, Carranza did not carry out all his promises and fighting continued between his forces and Zapata's supporters. Finally, Zapata was assassinated in 1919, and Carranza was assassinated the following year. By 1923, Villa had also been assassinated. In total between one and two million people had either been killed or had fled the country during the Revolution.

▼ This detail from Diego Rivera's mural depicting the history of Mexico shows leaders of the Revolution, including Emiliano Zapata, who is behind the banner at the back.

FROM REVOLUTION TO THE TWENTY-FIRST CENTURY

Between 1934 and 1940, oil nationalization, land reform and industrial expansion benefited many Mexicans. Later, between 1946 and 1970, industrial production grew steadily. However, during the 1960s, Mexican oil reserves began to run out, oil was imported and prices rose. Economic and political problems led to anti-government protests, which were often brutally suppressed. In 1968, hundreds were killed or injured when security forces fired on a demonstration in Mexico City. Further economic and political crises occurred in the 1980s and 1990s, including a 1994 uprising of indigenous people in Chiapas, protesting against inequality.

For just over seventy years, from 1929, the country was controlled by the PRI, or the Partido Revolucionario Institucional (the Institutional Revolutionary Party). The PRI had originally been formed to unite the victors of the revolution. At first, it had popular support, but from the 1970s onwards there was evidence that bribery and fraud were being used to keep the party in power. The PRI's dominance ended in 2000 when the opposition party won the presidential election. However, the PRI remained dominant in the Congress.

Focus on: The haciendas

During Porfirio Diaz's rule, large country estates, called haciendas, were owned by a few wealthy people. The haciendas were huge – one of them, in the northern state of Chihuahua, was as big as Belgium – and the landowners grew cash crops such as coffee or sisal. Local people provided the labour, working long, hard hours. In 1910, the revolutionary leader Emiliano Zapata demanded that the haciendas be divided up and given to the peasants. Most of the estates were eventually broken up, although some wealthy landowners managed to retain control of the property.

▶ The Castle of Chapultepec, Mexico City, was once the residence of Emperor Maximilian, ruler of Mexico from 1864 to 1867, and Lázaro Cárdenas, Mexican president from 1934 to 1940.

CHAPTER 3

Landscape and Climate

Mexico covers an area of 1,923,040 square kilometres (742,486 square miles), third in size after Argentina and Brazil in Latin America, and about four times the size of France. It shares a border with the United States to the north and with Belize and Guatemala to the south. To the west is the Pacific Ocean, and to the east is the Gulf of Mexico (part of the Caribbean). Within this large country, there are very varied physical landscapes and climates, including desert, tropical rainforest and temperate forest, providing different habitats for flora and fauna.

MOUNTAINS AND BEACHES

Two of the most striking landscape features in Mexico are the great mountain ranges, the Sierra Madre Occidental and the Sierra Madre Oriental. These ranges both run north to south, parallel with the Pacific and Gulf coasts. Between the two Sierra mountain ranges is the Central Plateau. The southern section of the plateau contains valleys originally formed by ancient lakes about 39,000 years ago. One of these, the Valley of Mexico, is home to 20 per cent of the Mexican population. There are low-lying coastal areas in the south, with sandy beaches, rocky headlands and islets, mangrove swamps, and even an offshore coral reef at Quintana Roo. Mexico's coastline is over 9,330 km (5,794 miles) in length – significantly longer than the coastline of any other Latin American country.

◀ Playa del Carmen, at Quintana Roo, is typical of the fine white-sand beaches found along the Caribbean coastline of the Yucatán Peninsula. Just offshore is the second-longest coral reef in the world. The beaches, the coral reef and the warm waters attract a variety of sealife, including dolphins and turtles.

WHERE THE PLATES OF THE EARTH'S CRUST MEET

Mexico is on the edge of one of the most dynamic tectonic areas in the world. The Pacific Ocean is surrounded by boundaries where plates that make up the Earth's crust meet each other. Along these boundaries are many of the world's volcanoes, which is why this area is known as the Pacific 'Ring of Fire'. One of the boundaries runs down the Pacific coast of Mexico, with Baja California lying along the famous San Andreas Fault. Further north, this fault runs through San Francisco in the United States. Volcanoes, earthquakes and tsunamis have all occurred in Mexico in the past. The most serious earthquake in recent times, measuring 8.1 on the Richter scale, caused devastation in Mexico City in 1985. More than 20,000 people were killed, many of them living in inner-city, multi-storey apartment blocks that collapsed during the earthquake.

▲ The volcano Popocatépetl is the second-highest peak in Mexico, standing at 5,465 m (17,930 feet).

 Did you know?

The Copper Canyon, in the Sierra Madre Occidental, is deeper than the Grand Canyon in the USA.

Focus on: Volcano Popocatépetl

The volcano Popocatépetl and the neighbouring peak of Iztaccihuatl can be seen from Mexico City (smog permitting!). As two of Mexico's highest peaks, often capped with snow, they are spectacular to look at. In December 2000, 'Popo', as the volcano is known to locals, erupted for the first time since the 1920s. This was a relatively small eruption with no reported fatalities but 56,000 were evacuated. A major eruption could threaten 30 million people living in the area.

INFLUENCES ON THE CLIMATE

Mexico has a number of different climatic zones, according to latitude, altitude and proximity to the sea. Half of Mexico lies south of the Tropic of Cancer and this region tends to be hot and humid. In the north of the country, there are also high temperatures but the climate tends to be much drier, mainly because the prevailing winds have already lost their moisture before they reach northern Mexico. Near the coasts, the influence of the sea can be felt. For example, the cold Californian sea current lowers temperatures and rainfall on the Pacific coast. Meanwhile, on the Gulf of Mexico coast, there are warm waters, which give a tropical climate. Inland, higher-altitude, mountainous areas tend to have lower temperatures and increased rainfall. Apart from a rainy season, which moves from south to north from May to October, there is generally little variation.

EFFECTS OF THE CLIMATE ON PEOPLE AND VEGETATION

Between June and November, parts of the Gulf of Mexico coast are likely to be affected by hurricanes, which run in from the Caribbean. Hurricanes also occur, less frequently, along the Pacific coast. The hurricane winds can lead to loss of life and cause considerable damage to property, and the heavy rain may cause mudslides and flooding on the mountainsides. However, the high rainfall in the highland areas replenishes reservoirs, providing much-needed water for urban areas and agriculture. The generally high temperatures also help attract tourists to the country.

The variations in Mexico's climate are reflected in the many different types of vegetation found throughout the country. In the arid region of the north, only drought-resistant plants such as cacti can survive. In the more temperate and humid zones, there are over 20,000 species of flowering plants. At the higher altitudes inland, there are mixed forests, including Montezuma pines, oaks and cypresses. Also, to the south, towards the coast of the Gulf of Mexico, are the last remaining areas of tropical rainforest in Mexico.

◀ Over half of Mexico is classified as arid, which means that it receives less than 100 mm (4 inches) of rainfall per year. Cacti, such as this one grown on Tiburon Island in the Gulf of California, have adapted to the dry conditions.

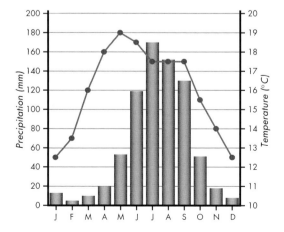 Many of Mexico's rainforest areas have been cleared for farming. This is one of the few remaining forests, in Oaxaca, southern Mexico.

▲ Average monthly climate conditions in Mexico City

 Did you know?

About 75 per cent of Mexico is mountainous, with much of this high terrain over 1,000 m (3,280 feet) above sea level. The country's highest peak is Pico de Orizaba at 5,700 m (18,700 feet).

 Did you know?

Temperatures below freezing are not uncommon above 3,000 m (9,842 feet) in the Mexican part of the Sierra mountain ranges, and there is permanent snow on the loftiest peaks. The highest temperatures are experienced in northern Mexico. In the desert regions of the north-east, the average July temperature is 35°C (95°F) and a maximum of 47°C (117°F) has been recorded for Guaymas in the north-west.

CHAPTER 4

Population and Settlements

Mexico has a total population of about 104.9 million. The population has increased from only 12 million in 1900, with the most rapid growth (3.5 per cent each year) in the 1960s. The population is still growing, but at a slower rate of about 1.5 per cent each year (which is still relatively high). Life expectancy has generally increased, with a particularly noticeable drop in infant mortality because of improved health and medicine. As a result of these trends, young people under 25 make up half the population. Some sections of society, mostly indigenous peoples, still have high death and high infant mortality rates because of poverty and poor living conditions.

A DIVERSE PEOPLE

Mexico's population is very diverse. It has the largest number of different indigenous peoples in any Latin American country. These peoples, who are descended from the ancient civilizations, such as the Mayas, include many different groupings, with approximately 60 indigenous languages still being spoken. The majority of Mexicans are *mestizo* (of mixed Indian and Spanish descent).

▼ A Mexican family, with young children, sits down to a meal at home. Mexico has a youthful population compared to many countries that are more economically developed.

MOVEMENT INTO AND OUT OF MEXICO

People migrate into Mexico in the south from the relatively poor countries of Guatemala and El Salvador, many doing so illegally. Some stay in Mexico but for many the goal is to travel north, through Mexico, and into the United States. Crossing this southern border into

▲ The Mayas, one of the many indigenous groups of Mexico, live in the Yucatán region.

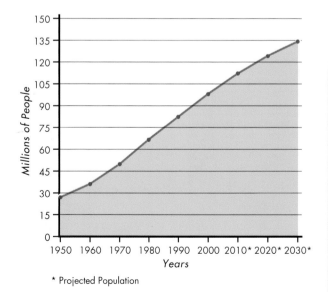

* Projected Population

▲ Population growth 1950-2030

Population data

📂 Population: 104.9 million

📂 Population 0-14 yrs: 32%

📂 Population 15-64 yrs: 63%

📂 Population 65+ yrs: 5%

📂 Population growth rate (2000-2005): 1.5%

📂 Population density: 54.5 per sq km/141.3 per sq mile

📂 Urban population: 76%

📂 Major cities: Mexico City 19,013,000 Guadalajara 3,905,000, Monterrey 3,517,000

Sources: United Nations and World Bank

Mexico illegally is incredibly risky. Attempts to jump onto moving freight trains under cover of darkness often result in injury or even death. The chances of being caught by the Mexican police are also high, with over 150,000 people being detained and sent back each year. In Mexico's north, large numbers of people migrate over the border into the USA, both legally and illegally.

MOVEMENT WITHIN MEXICO

Mexico's population is unevenly distributed. About 20 per cent of its people live in the Valley of Mexico, which is an area of only 330 sq km (127 sq miles). Since the 1980s, many people have moved in search of jobs in the industrial towns of northern Mexico. These towns are on or near the border with the United States and are home to thousands of *maquiladoras* (factories where goods are manufactured for sale in the USA). Many Mexicans are eager to work in these factories because the wage rates are higher than elsewhere in the country. Within Mexico, these northern towns, such as Tijuana and Ciudad Juárez, are now among the fastest-growing settlements in the country.

Over the past fifty years, increasing migration from the countryside has led to the numbers living in towns and cities almost doubling. Now, over 75 per cent of Mexico's population live in urban areas. Many migrants move to

◀ The majority of Mexicans live in overcrowded industrial towns, like Guanajuato (shown here).

Focus on: Illegal migration into the USA

As US immigration officials patrol much of the Mexican/US border, illegal migrants aim to cross where they are less likely to be detected. Many used to struggle across the Rio Bravo/Rio Grande river, which led to them being called 'wetbacks' as an insult. However, since 1994, when Operation Gatekeeper was introduced by US President Bill Clinton, the river has been more tightly patrolled, so the migrants head for the sparsely populated desert of Arizona. Whereas many used to drown in their attempts to cross the river, about 500 are now thought to die each year from thirst and heat exhaustion. Those who do survive are still likely to be arrested, as over a million Mexicans are detained yearly in the United States, before being sent back to Mexico. However, as they tend to be from the poorest sections of Mexican society, these illegal migrants are likely to try again because they believe that being resident in the USA will give them access to a better standard of living, with well-paid jobs, educational opportunities and good healthcare.

Mexico City because it is both the capital and the largest city, being approximately five times bigger than Guadalajara, the next-largest city in Mexico.

Mexico City attracts people because they believe there will be more job opportunities and their quality of life will be better. However, when they get there, the reality may be quite different. The lack of adequate housing in Mexico City means that many migrants end up living in shanty towns without clean water or sanitation facilities. This is also true of those moving to other cities such as Guadalajara and to the northern industrial towns, where conditions are often very poor, with too few facilities for the numbers living there.

Many small farmers are leaving rural areas because soil erosion has left them with no good land to farm. There are also problems with land ownership. Although one of the main aims of the Mexican Revolution was to give everyone equal access to land, much of the land is still concentrated in the hands of a few rich landowners. In the years immediately following the Mexican Revolution, many of the large estates were split up and smaller parcels of land were given to landless peasants in the local communities. Over the years, these parcels of land have been divided up to be passed on to children of farmers and now 60 per cent of them are 2 hectares (5 acres) or less in size, which is too little to provide a living.

 Did you know?

The population of Mexico City has grown from 16,790,000 in 1995 to 19,013,000 in 2005. This is the equivalent of adding 609 people every day over the 10-year period.

▼ In rural Mexico, there are many small, scattered settlements, such as this one in the desert state of Coahuila.

CHAPTER 5

Government and Politics

Mexico is a federal republic with 31 states and the federal district of Mexico City. The president is both head of the government and head of state, which is a symbolic role representing Mexico in the international community. The country is governed by the National Congress, made up of the Senate (with 128 senators) and the Federal Chamber of Deputies (with 500 deputies). The senators and deputies, who are democratically elected by citizens over 18, represent the states that make up the federal republic. Presidential elections are held every six years, and an individual president can only serve one term.

DEMOCRACY AND CORRUPTION

Mexico has supposedly been a democracy since the establishment of the Mexican federal republic in 1824. However, from 1929 until 2000, the country was effectively a one-party state. The Partido Revolucionario Institucional (PRI), originally formed in 1929, won all elections. Until the 1970s, they won as a result of popularity, but later, when voters became disillusioned by the country's economic problems, they won by suppressing official opposition, and corruption was widespread. Not surprisingly, the defeat of the PRI's presidential candidate in 2000 was seen as a major turning point in Mexico's history. Since then, the new government, headed by Vicente Fox of the National Action Party, has been trying to tackle the problems of corruption and political repression. Congress is also playing a more important role and has gained more power to balance that of the president.

◀ A giant national flag flies in the Zócalo, Mexico City's main square. Mexicans are now enjoying a reasonably stable period after the political turbulence of the past.

The Constitution, laying down the rights and duties of Mexican citizens, dates from 1917 and was drawn up to meet the demands of the Revolution for freedom and equal rights. Although equality is still held to be important, in reality certain groups in Mexican society wield more power than others. For example, many indigenous peoples in Mexico feel their rights are not recognized and this led to anti-government protests in Chiapas State in 1994. Women also hold only 5 per cent of decision-making positions in government. There is official commitment to the improvement of this situation but progress has been slow.

Focus on: Indian uprising in Chiapas

In 1994, the Ejército Zapatista de Liberación Nacional (Zapatista National Liberation Army, or EZLN) led armed uprisings of the Indian people in Chiapas State in southern Mexico, calling for greater recognition of Indians' rights. The indigenous people here were among the poorest in Mexico. They feared that Mexico's signing of the North American Free Trade Agreement (NAFTA) was going to make them poorer, by attracting even more business to the north of Mexico, which is geographically closer to the USA. They were also concerned that the NAFTA would lead to cheap US agricultural goods competing with those produced by farmers in the Chiapas region. Following fighting between the rebels and government troops, a ceasefire was called and has been in place ever since. In 2001, new legislation was passed, giving indigenous people more rights. However, the EZLN does not believe that this legislation went far enough in promoting Indian rights and so they have continued their political campaign non-violently.

▼ People fishing near a border patrol post at Ojinaga, one of many such posts set up on the US side of the Rio Bravo (or Rio Grande, as it is called in the USA) to combat the problem of Mexican economic migrants trying to enter the USA illegally.

MEXICO'S RELATIONSHIP WITH THE USA

Mexico and the United States have strong economic links. They are both members, along with Canada, of the North American Free Trade Agreement (NAFTA), formed in 1994. NAFTA promotes trade between its member countries and has eased the movement of goods and money between them. Mexico and the USA also agree on many foreign policy issues. For example, both governments co-operate closely in trying to eradicate drug trafficking over the Mexican-US border. However, they take very different approaches to the problem of illegal immigration from Mexico to the USA. The Mexican government favours the introduction of temporary visas, which would allow migrants to move to the USA for short periods and cross back to visit their families, while the USA is more inclined to tighten up border controls because of worries that there would be a huge influx of poor people from Mexico.

▼ People wait in their cars at a US inspection station at Tijuana, on the Mexican-US border, one of the world's busiest border crossing points.

The Mexican and US governments also co-operate with each other in tackling environmental issues that affect both sides of the border. Several decision-making bodies, such as the International Boundary and Water Commission and the Border Environment Co-operation Commission (BECC), have equal numbers of Mexican and US delegates. Through these bodies, joint projects have been undertaken on problems related to water supply, waste disposal, air quality and the protection of shared habitats, such as the deserts of Sonora/Arizona.

 Did you know?

In 1967, the then Mexican president, Gustavo Diaz Ordaz, initiated the drafting of a treaty prohibiting any Latin American and Caribbean country from acquiring nuclear weapons. The Treaty of Tlatelolco, named after the district in Mexico City where it was drafted, has now been signed by all 33 Latin American and Caribbean countries.

A MEMBER OF THE INTERNATIONAL COMMUNITY

Mexico has diplomatic relations with over 170 countries and is a member of several international organizations. Mexico was one of the first countries to join the United Nations (UN) when the UN was formed in 1945. In 1994, Mexico also became the first Latin American country to join the Organization for Economic Co-operation and Development (OECD), set up in 1961. Mexico has trade agreements with other Latin American countries (Guatemala, Honduras, El Salvador) and with the European Union (EU), in an attempt to balance its dependence on the USA, which buys almost 90 per cent of Mexico's exports. Mexico was also a founding member of the World Trade Organization (WTO), established in 1995.

▼ The port of Veracruz plays a vital role in Mexico's import and export trade, handling many different cargoes, including textiles, iron, steel and chemicals.

CHAPTER 6

Energy and Resources

Mexico is the fifth-largest producer of oil in the world, although it is not a member of the Organization of Petroleum Exporting Countries (OPEC). Major oil reserves were first found in the 1880s but began to run dry, and by 1971 Mexico was importing oil. Big new reserves were discovered in the mid-1970s and these have continued to provide Mexico with oil, both for its own needs and to export to other countries. As oil is a major source of income for Mexico, and the state oil company PEMEX provides about one-third of government revenue, world oil prices directly affect Mexico's economy. During the 1970s, oil accounted for 78 per cent of all Mexican exports. Then, in 1981, world oil prices dropped, and Mexico's income fell drastically and it was unable to pay back money it had borrowed from foreign investors. Since then, Mexico has tried to make its economy more balanced by developing its manufacturing and tourism industries.

GAS RESERVES

Natural gas is also produced, mainly in the south of the country. However, until recently, it has not been used to meet the country's energy needs. Now the Mexican government wants to develop the use of natural gas, because it is a cleaner fuel than oil, and they aim to double its use by 2010. Increased use of gas will require more refineries and more pipelines to transport it from the south to the north where industrial demand for energy is higher. Until these refineries and pipelines can be constructed, Mexico continues to import natural gas from the USA for use in the north.

◀ PEMEX, Mexico's state-owned oil company, was established in 1938. It owns all the country's filling stations.

▲ Gas being flared off at an oil refinery in Tampico. Gas vapours are a by-product of oil drilling, and they are flared in order to dispose of them.

ELECTRICITY GENERATION

Around 92 per cent of Mexico's electricity is generated from oil, gas and coal, 1 per cent from hydro-electricity, 1 per cent from nuclear power plants, and 6 per cent from renewable sources. With continued industrial development, a rising population and increasing use of electricity in homes, electricity consumption is steadily increasing. In fact, demand may very soon outstrip supply.

There are plans to produce more electricity, including the development of renewable sources. Hydro-electric power (HEP) has been an important source in the past but drought conditions in northern Mexico have caused serious problems with this form of electricity generation. Other sources to be expanded are geothermal, solar and wind power. The

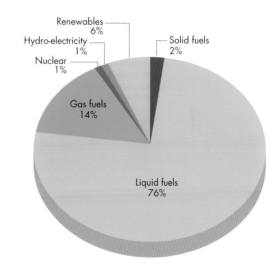

Renewables 6%
Hydro-electricity 1%
Nuclear 1%
Solid fuels 2%
Gas fuels 14%
Liquid fuels 76%

▲ Energy use by type

 Did you know?

Mexico has very high levels of potential geothermal energy, which is derived from natural heat in the Earth's crust. At present, the country utilizes approximately 955 megawatts of geothermal energy but it has been estimated that this could be expanded to 8,000 megawatts.

government now seems to be recognizing the advantages of these renewable forms of energy. Wind power plants are being set up in Oaxaca.

Energy data

- Energy consumption as % of world total:1.4%
- Energy consumption by sector (% of total)

Industry:	41
Transportation:	38
Agriculture:	2
Services:	3
Residential:	16

- CO_2 emissions as % of world total: 1.5
- CO_2 emissions per capita p.a.: 3.7 tonnes (3.64 tons)

Source: World Resources Institute

MINERALS AND METALS

Largely owing to the intense seismic activity that affects the region, Mexico is very rich in minerals, including silver, gold, copper, lead, tungsten, iron ore and zinc. However, only about 5 per cent of the country's mineral reserves have been exploited so far, partly because of lack of investment and partly because of the difficulty of extracting mineral deposits in mountainous terrain.

Mexico is the world's largest producer of silver (producing about 14 per cent of the world's yearly total), and silver production provides about 2 per cent of Mexico's gross domestic product (GDP). Until its closure in 1998, the largest silver mine in the world was at Real de Angeles, with an output of 10,000 tonnes

▶ Gold has been mined in Mexico for centuries. Here, a miner drills for gold in a mine tunnel at Durango, in central Mexico.

(9,842 tons) of ore a day, from which 220 tonnes (216.5 tons) of silver could be extracted. Production continues at other mines, including Fresnillo, in Zacatecas State. Much of the silver produced is exported, mainly to the USA, although some is retained for Mexican use.

OTHER RICHES FROM THE LAND AND SEA

Timber is an important resource, including hardwoods, such as mahogany, and softwoods, such as pine. However, large-scale commercial forestry has led to extensive areas becoming deforested, with 770,000 hectares (1,902,643 acres) per year having been cleared between 1993 and 2000. This problem is beginning to be addressed with re-planting schemes and an emphasis on more sustainable use. Fishing also

provides a valuable source of income for inhabitants of some coastal and lakeside settlements. The main catches from the Pacific include lobsters, sardines and anchovies, while the Gulf of Mexico and the Caribbean provide shrimp, snape, mackerel and mullet.

The commercial potential of Mexico's wonderfully diverse landscapes and wildlife is increasingly being recognized, with major developments in eco-tourism and adventure tourism. With more than 26,000 plant species (including cacti and orchids), almost 450 different mammals (such as elephant seals, the Mexican bighorn sheep and black bears) and over 1,000 species of birds (including hummingbirds, eagles and pelicans), there is much to appeal to anyone with an interest in nature. Mexico's varied natural environments also offer opportunities for outdoor activities such as climbing, hiking and white-water rafting.

▼ Mexico's indigenous people have always fished the seas around the Baja California coastline.

Focus on: Community Forestry Project

The Community Forestry Project, funded by the World Bank, is an example of how small local communities in Mexico are being helped to conserve their forest resources and protect endangered species. Over 500 indigenous communities have received money and technical assistance to develop alternative sources of income that are sustainable. For instance, some groups have set up shade-grown coffee co-operatives where the forest canopy of valuable tropical tree species is maintained, rather than felling trees for timber.

CHAPTER 7

Economy and Income

Mexico is now considered to be a middle economy country by the World Bank, meaning that its Gross National Income (GNI) is higher than that of less developed countries but lower than fully industrialized ones such as the United States and the UK. The development of a range of industries, including car and electronics manufacture, has contributed to Mexico becoming one of the strongest economies in Latin America. Guadalajara, the capital of the central state of Jalisco (known as the Mexican 'Silicon Valley'), is a centre for the production of high-tech electronic goods and has helped to make Mexico one of the world leaders in this field.

Tourism has become a major source of employment in Mexico and the third most important source of foreign income, following oil and remittances (money sent back by migrant workers, mainly in the USA). In terms of employment, the manufacturing and service industries have developed over recent years, while agriculture has shrunk. However, all sectors contribute to the economy by means of the money earned from exports.

FREE TRADE WITH THE USA

In 1994, Mexico signed the North American Free Trade Agreement (NAFTA) with the United States and Canada, with the aim of eliminating all trade tariffs by 2010. Since then, trade between these countries has tripled. In many ways, Mexico has benefited from being part of NAFTA. For example, its economy grew by over 5 per cent per year in 1999 and 2000. Mexico is now the USA's second largest trading partner (Canada is the largest), with 88 per cent of Mexico's exports

◀ With plenty of sandy beaches and luxurious hotels, Cancún (in the Yucatán region) is popular with wealthy Mexicans as well as foreign tourists.

going to the United States. This close relationship has obviously stimulated certain sectors of the economy, such as the manufacture of electronic goods and the production of crops such as tomatoes. However, being so strongly linked to the US economy does have its problems, and this was demonstrated in 2001 when an economic downturn in the USA resulted in no growth in the Mexican economy. The economic benefits of the trading links with the USA have also been largely concentrated in north and central Mexico, leaving the south behind.

WOMEN IN THE WORKFORCE

Women made up 37 per cent of Mexico's workforce in 2002. This percentage has more than doubled over 20 years, partly because of new attitudes introduced by the feminist movement, which encouraged women to become economically independent. Another reason for the increase in female workers was the economic hardship that Mexico experienced during the 1980s, which meant that women, as

Economic data

- ▷ Gross National Income (GNI) in US$: 637,159,200,000
- ▷ World rank by GNI: 10
- ▷ GNI per capita in US$: 6,230
- ▷ World rank by GNI per capita: 68
- ▷ Economic growth: 1%

Source: World Bank

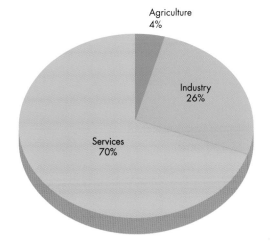

▲ Contribution by sector to national income

Agriculture 4%
Industry 26%
Services 70%

Did you know?

Mexico now produces 98 per cent of the televisions in North America.

▶ Maize is the main agricultural product and a staple food of Mexico. It is grown on a large-scale commercial basis and also by subsistence farmers for their own consumption.

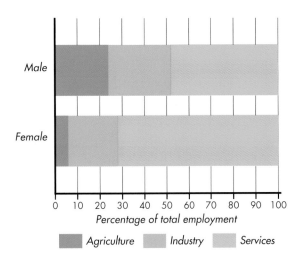

Percentage of total employment

Agriculture   Industry   Services

▲ Labour force by sector and gender

INEQUALITY AND POVERTY

Mexico has one of the most unequal distributions of wealth in the world, with 20 per cent of the population owning 55 per cent of the wealth. In 2000, 23 million Mexicans were living in extreme poverty, at times unable to afford even essential food. Poverty is mainly concentrated in the rural south, where there are fewer industries and smaller farms. Poverty is also a problem for small-scale farmers in the north who depend on irrigation systems, as they cannot afford to run these systems efficiently, and for many residents of the rapidly growing cities in the north and south.

well as men, needed to bring in money to make ends meet. (Until this time, men had traditionally been the breadwinners.) Since the 1980s, more married women have been working instead of devoting themselves to home and children. However, in Mexico, women still earn less than men. For example, in manufacturing industries their wages are 30 per cent lower than men's wages.

These economic problems are not easy to solve. Many poor Mexicans leave their homes to migrate to the USA, in the hope of improving their income and quality of life. Once in the USA, they often find jobs, although these are

▼ Poor farmers in rural areas, as shown here in the state of Veracruz, still use donkeys as their main means of transport.

generally poorly paid. Much of their income is sent back to their families and these payments (known as remittances) are one of the biggest sources of foreign income for Mexico. The government is trying to deal with rural poverty and, in association with the World Bank, has drawn up the Development Strategy for the Mexican Southern States, the region that is home to 25 per cent of all Mexicans living in extreme poverty.

Focus on: Quality of life in the border region

▲ Four *maquiladora* workers in Tijuana have a break at lunchtime, before returning for their afternoon shift.

The northern region, running along the 3,153 km (1,958 mile) border with the USA, is the most rapidly developing area in Mexico. It has the highest rates of industrial growth and employment. Over the past twenty years, more than 3,000 factories have been built along the Mexican/US border. Know as *maquiladoras*, these factories manufacture goods for the US market. Many are owned by foreign companies who exploit the low wage rates of Mexican workers in order to increase their profits. The wages may be low by US standards but they are relatively high compared to wages elsewhere in Mexico. These factory jobs also offer permanent, regular income and have thus helped to strengthen the northern region's economy. However, there are also disadvantages. Since the signing of NAFTA in 1994, increases in the number of factories and the number of trucks transporting goods across the border have led to very high levels of air pollution. Although co-operation between Mexico and the USA has been successful in tackling some environmental issues in this region, such as treatment of waste water, problems with household waste disposal and water supplies still endanger the health of the local population.

CHAPTER 8

Global Connections

Mexico has trade links with many countries. Its major trading commitment is the North American Free Trade Agreement (NAFTA) with the USA and Canada. The country also has free trade agreements with the European Union (EU) and with other Latin American countries. Mexico is a member of the Organization for Economic Co-operation and Development (OECD), the Asia-Pacific Economic Co-operation forum (APEC), and was a founding member of the World Trade Organization (WTO). Each of these organizations offers opportunities for dealing with trading disputes by negotiation. And the OECD also provides a forum for the consideration of economic development issues such as the impact of industry on the environment.

CROSSING THE BORDER

The border between Mexico and the USA is one of the few places in the world where a highly economically developed country and a less economically developed one share a land boundary. This economic difference is reflected in the relationship between Mexico and the USA. The wealthier USA attracts migrants from Mexico, many of whom are prepared to risk crossing the border illegally in search of work and a better quality of life. Although there are problems associated with the very large numbers of migrants coming into the USA, many of them provide a source of cheap labour and do menial jobs that no one else wants. Others may do skilled work or start their own businesses. There is also a movement of people from the USA into Mexico, but more for recreation than work: over 80 per cent of tourists visiting Mexico come from the USA. Manufactured goods cross the border in both

◀ Traders outside the Stock Market building in Mexico City. Mexico plays a very active role in global financial markets.

directions. Goods imported from Mexico tend to be cheaper than those produced in the USA because of the low Mexican wage rates. At the same time, there are approximately 30 million better-off Mexicans who want to buy imported US and Canadian manufactured goods.

FINANCIAL HELP

Despite the wealth generated by its oil and other exports, Mexico still needs money from the global community to tackle its problems of poverty. Mexico therefore receives international aid in the form of loans from the World Bank. In order to obtain funding and technical expertise for development schemes, the Mexican government needs to work in co-operation with the World Bank and to show a commitment to dealing with economic problems through its own development policies.

▶ A nodding-donkey oil well in Poza Rica. As well as small onshore facilities like this one, there are huge off-shore rigs on the extensive oil fields in the Gulf of Mexico.

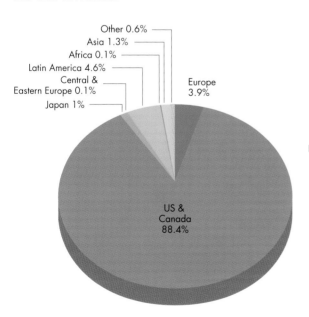

Other 0.6%
Asia 1.3%
Africa 0.1%
Latin America 4.6%
Central & Eastern Europe 0.1%
Japan 1%
Europe 3.9%
US & Canada 88.4%

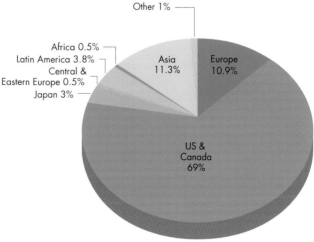

Other 1%
Africa 0.5%
Latin America 3.8%
Central & Eastern Europe 0.5%
Japan 3%
Asia 11.3%
Europe 10.9%
US & Canada 69%

▲ Destinations of exports by major trading region

▲ Origin of imports by major trading region

PARTICIPATION IN THE INTERNATIONAL COMMUNITY

As a country with considerable biodiversity and an industrializing economy, Mexico faces many environmental protection issues. The country plays an important role in international environmental negotiations and has ratified over 100 international environmental agreements.

Mexico was one of the first countries to join the United Nations (UN), following its creation in 1945. As a member of the UN, Mexico is committed to world peace through international co-operation and respect for human rights. Nevertheless, the Mexican government has sometimes been guilty of human rights violations. During the 1970s and 1980s, for example, many left-wing opponents of the government mysteriously disappeared. When evidence from files kept by the security forces was made public in 2001, it showed these activists to have been abducted, tortured and killed. President Vicente Fox then commissioned an investigation and, in 2002,

three army officers were charged with murder. This was a step towards fulfilling the promise the President made when he was elected in 2000 – to promote human rights and to increase Mexico's participation in international affairs.

? Did you know?

Although Mexico has chosen not to become a member of the Organization of Petroleum Exporting Countries (OPEC), Mexican representatives still attend most of OPEC's meetings. Mexico has also sometimes worked with OPEC to influence world oil supplies. For example, in 2002 Mexico pledged to limit its exports to 1.66 million barrels per day (a cut of 100,000 barrels per day) for six months in order to stop oil prices from falling.

▼ All the main American fast-food chains can be found in Mexico's cities. Individual street vendors, such as this one in Veracruz, are also influenced by the demand for American-style fast food.

A CULTURE UNDER THREAT?

Mexico and the United States have often been described as having a love-hate relationship. Some Mexicans are becoming concerned that aspects of American culture are starting to undermine Mexican traditions. For example, highly commercialized Halloween celebrations are threatening to replace the traditional Day of the Dead festivities. Likewise, American fast-food outlets, selling items such as burgers, hot dogs, pizzas and fries, are spreading into Mexican towns and cities, and most films showing in Mexican cinemas are made in Hollywood. However, Mexico's cultural influence has also spread beyond its own borders. For instance, Mexican cuisine has become one of the most popular foreign foods in developed countries such as the United States and the UK, while Tex-Mex food incorporates influences from both sides of the Mexican-US border.

Focus on: The Mexican film industry

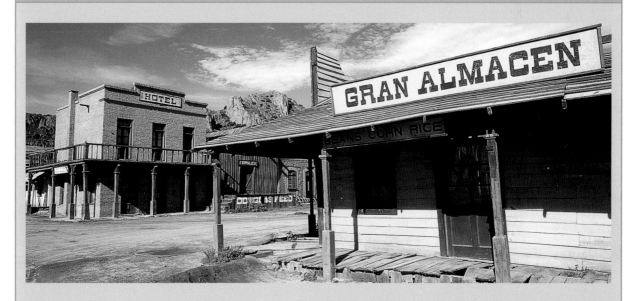

▲ The main street of Capuaderos, Durango, where many Western movies have been filmed.

From the 1920s to the 1950s, Mexico had a thriving film industry with its own studio and star system, producing about 150 films a year. However, the Mexican film industry has since faded away and Hollywood has taken over. In 1998, only 10 films were made in Mexico. This has not only led to a loss of employment and status but has also made it difficult for Mexican film directors to portray the rich diversity of Mexican society. Meanwhile, films made in Hollywood tend to stereotype Mexicans as poor, corrupt and violent. In an attempt to revitalize the national film industry, the Mexican Congress passed a law stating that 10 per cent of Mexican cinema screens must show Mexican-made films. Although the number of films made in Mexico rose to 30 in 2000, there is still not enough investment in Mexican films to enable the industry to recapture its former glory.

CHAPTER 9

Transport and Communications

Mexico has the most extensive road network in Latin America. However, the quality of the roads varies enormously, with a mix of paved and unpaved. Paved roads have increased considerably over recent years, from 85,000 km (52,785 miles) in the mid-1990s to 108,087 km (67,122 miles) in 2002, although many are poorly maintained. The main highways, linking cities and crossing into the USA, tend to be of better quality and are used by freight trucks and inter-city buses as well as private cars.

The Inter-American Highway, a section of the Pan-American Highway, runs 5,470 km (3,397 miles) down the country, from Nuevo Laredo on the US border to Panama City, Panama. This highway links Mexico with Alaska to the north and Argentina to the south, although there is a break of approximately 97 km (60 miles) south of Mexico.

▼ A busy highway in Monterrey. Road transport dominates in Mexico, taking 95 per cent of passenger traffic and 80 per cent of freight.

TRAVELLING BY RAIL, AIR AND SEA

Mexico's railway system is concentrated in the northern and central areas, though much of the country is too mountainous for railway track to be built. There are numerous connections with the USA and a connection with Central American networks through Guatemala. The railway system is in great need of modernization, with most of its rolling stock dating from the 1950s. Because of the rail network's inefficiency, few passengers use trains and very little freight is carried by rail.

Mexico has 1,827 airports. Of these, 231 have paved runways and are able to take large commercial aircraft. Mexico is the destination and starting point for many international flights, with growing numbers of passengers arriving and departing as the tourist industry expands. Mexican airports also handle many domestic flights.

The Mexican coastline has no natural harbours but several ocean ports have been constructed. The east coast ports include Veracruz (used for cargo), and Tampico, Coatzacoalcos, and Progesso (used for petroleum). The principal ports on the Pacific coast are Guaymas, Mazatlán and Manzanillo. These ports used to be run by the state and had a reputation for inefficiency. Then, in 1993, the ports were sold to private companies and there has since been an overall growth in freight, with 1.7 million containers being handled nationally in 2003. There are several fishing ports around the coasts, although 75 per cent of Mexico's catch comes through ports on the Pacific coast.

 Did you know?

One of the most scenic railway routes in the world, the Chihuahua al Pacifico, runs from the USA, down through the Copper Canyon, to the Pacific coast. Work began on the line's construction in the 1870s. It has 86 tunnels and 37 bridges and it was not completed until 1961. The line is now mainly used by tourists.

▼ A train station on the scenic line that runs through the Copper Canyon. Nowadays, most of the line's passengers are sightseers.

TRANSPORT IN URBAN AND RURAL AREAS

Traffic congestion and air pollution caused by vehicle emissions are particularly pressing problems in Mexico City because of the huge numbers of people who live and work there. The subway system, opened in 1969, is one of the busiest in the world, with more than 12 million passengers using it every day. Car and bus use have outgrown the capacity of the roads, leading to almost continuous traffic jams. At any one time, there are over 5 million drivers attempting to drive their vehicles along the capital city's roads.

In rural areas, local buses are the most common form of transport. Bicycles also provide a relatively cheap way to move around. Farmers may have tractors, although these are likely to be old, and some still depend on outdated forms of transport such as donkey carts.

Transport and communications

- Total roads: 329,532 km/204,639 miles
- Total paved roads: 108,087 km/ 67,122 miles
- Total unpaved roads: 221,445 km/ 137,517 miles
- Total railways: 19,510 km/12,116 miles
- Major airports: 231
- Cars per 1,000 people: 107
- Mobile phones per 1,000 people: 255
- Personal computers per 1,000 people: 82
- Internet users per 1,000 people: 98

Sources: World Bank and CIA World Factbook

▼ Bicycles are often used to carry passengers and parcels as well as individual riders, as shown here in the Yucatán region.

Focus on: Air quality in Mexico City

Mexico City's smog problem is particularly severe because most of the residents' vehicles are old and poorly maintained and also because the city's location, in a valley with mountains on three sides, causes pollutants to become trapped in the air. Various anti-pollution measures have been taken, including fitting all cars with catalytic converters and restricting entry to the city on 'No Drive Days'. (On a specified day of the week, vehicles with a particular digit at the end of their registration numbers are banned from entering the city.) There has been some improvement and the air is now clear enough on most days to see the distant volcanoes. However, ozone and suspended particles still frequently reach levels that are considered hazardous to health. Future plans include the development of a rapid transit bus system, to encourage more people to use public transport and leave their cars at home.

▼ Heavy traffic in Mexico City. On smog alert days, schoolchildren are ordered to stay indoors.

MEDIA AND COMMUNICATIONS

As wealth has increased in northern and central Mexico, both radio and TV ownership have risen. Television was first introduced in 1950, and by the 1990s over 70 per cent of the population had access to at least one TV set. Many people listen to the radio and there are over 1,000 local and regional radio stations.

The number of telephone lines has increased, from 8.7 million in 1995 to about 16 million in 2003. Businesses and government offices are now connected to the national telephone network but many homes, particularly in poorer, rural neighbourhoods, do not have the necessary infrastructure. Mobile phone use is developing fast, with over 28 million users in 2003. Access to the Internet is also increasing, with over 10 million users in 2002. Mexico has a number of international communications facilities, including satellite earth stations and a high-capacity fibre-optic submarine cable linked to the USA, the Canary Islands, Spain, Morocco and Italy.

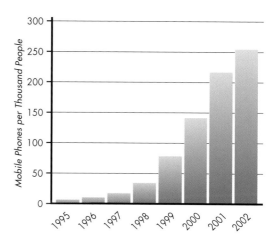

▲ Mobile phone use per 1,000 people, 1995-2002

CHAPTER 10

Education and Health

According to the Mexican Constitution, children are guaranteed free education from 6 to 14, and by 2008 this will be extended to include nursery education from the age of 3. However, while nearly all children enrol in school, fewer than 90 per cent actually complete primary education. Although state primary education is free, wealthier Mexicans still prefer to pay, and about 10 per cent of children attend private schools. Secondary education tends to focus on vocational and technical qualifications.

Universities, technical institutions and teacher training colleges provide higher education. There are both public and private universities. Private ones, only open to those with money, tend to offer better-quality facilities than the public ones. Teachers are generally highly regarded in Mexican society, though they are poorly paid. In order to earn enough money, many teachers have to work double shifts, sometimes travelling between two schools to do so, or they take on evening work such as driving taxis.

OBSTACLES TO EDUCATION

The school attendance of children from poorer and more isolated areas, many of them from indigenous groups, tends to be lower than the national average, often because they are needed at home to help with younger children or to go to work themselves. In addition, schools in these areas are not very well-equipped. Because of low attendance and poor educational facilities, the illiteracy rate for indigenous peoples is five times higher than the national average. Adult literacy programmes are available in poorer regions, particularly the rural south of the country. In the state of Chiapas, for example, 23.5 per cent of adults are illiterate, compared to Mexico

◀ In the 1950s, the National Autonomous University of Mexico, in Mexico City, moved to a campus. The campus has purpose-built facilities, such as this library with its mosaic by Juan O'Gorman depicting Mexico's scientific achievements.

City's rate of 3.1 per cent. In the country as a whole, literacy rates have improved steadily but there are still more literate men, with 92.6 per cent able to read and write, than women, with 88.7 per cent. Women have traditionally been seen as home-makers and this belief still reduces access to education for many girls. In the poorer urban areas of Mexico, a significant number of children drop out between the primary and secondary phases of education, as much as 66 per cent in some places. This high drop-out rate is partly linked to a lack of job prospects.

Did you know?

In 1970, the average length of schooling in Mexico was four years for men and three years for women. By 2003, the average length had risen to eight years for men and seven years for women.

Education and health data

- Life expectancy at birth male: 70.7
- Life expectancy at birth female: 76.7
- Infant mortality rate per 1,000: 24
- Under five mortality rate per 1,000: 29
- Physicians per 1,000 people: 1.5
- Health expenditure as % of GDP: 6.1%
- Education expenditure as % of GDP: 4.4%
- Primary net enrolment (1996-2002): 100%
- Pupil-teacher ratio, primary: 27.3
- Adult literacy as % age 15+: 90.5

Sources: United Nations Agencies and World Bank

▼ These secondary school students, in Los Mochis, are fortunate enough to have access to good-quality educational resources.

THE HEALTHCARE SYSTEM

With a lower GDP per capita, Mexico spends less on healthcare than wealthier countries. (For example, Mexico spends eight times less than the USA.) However, the number of doctors has increased significantly over the past ten years and the basic public health system is used by 75 per cent of the population. Better-quality healthcare can be bought by the wealthy. There are also health insurance schemes for those employed in organizations and businesses, and the Mexican government plans to improve the public healthcare system. To this end, schemes funded by the World Bank are targeting particular geographical areas of need, mainly in the south of the country.

HEALTH ISSUES

Life expectancy is relatively high and many childhood diseases have been eradicated, which has reduced the infant mortality rate (now nationally about 24 per 1,000 live births). Mexico has a very effective childhood immunization programme, with 95 per cent of children being vaccinated against measles (compared to the USA's rate of 91 per cent). In addition, 88 per cent of Mexicans now have access to disinfected water, resulting in a decrease in gastro-intestinal illnesses and the disappearance of cholera.

▼ A boy waits at a rural clinic in Chihuahua State. Rural areas tend to have poorer healthcare facilities than towns and cities.

However, not everyone benefits equally from these measures. Indigenous groups usually live in rural and sometimes quite remote areas. They tend to have poorer access to healthcare services and clean water and therefore suffer more health problems. Infant mortality rates are also higher among these groups. For example, in the poorest areas in the southern states the rate is as high as 203 per 1,000, compared to 9 per 1,000 in the richer parts of Mexico City.

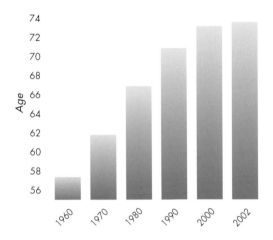

▲ Life expectancy at birth, 1960-2002

Rapidly growing urban areas, like Mexico City and the northern industrial towns such as Ciudad Juárez, also have some neighbourhoods that lack adequate water supplies and sanitation services. In addition, these urban areas have poor air quality because of heavy concentrations of vehicles emitting pollutants, resulting in a higher incidence of respiratory problems than in rural areas. It is thought that as much as one-third of Mexicans' respiratory problems are caused by air pollution.

▶ A Mayan Indian woman in Mérida. Groups such as the Mayas are more likely to suffer from health problems caused by their poor living conditions.

Focus on: 'Life style' health problems

Diseases linked to a high-fat and high-sugar diet, such as heart disease and certain cancers, are becoming more common in Mexico. Adult obesity is also increasing. According to a report published in 2003, around 24 per cent of Mexican adults were considered obese (a higher percentage than that of the UK but less than that of the USA at 33 per cent). This increase in obesity is likely to lead to a rise in diabetes (a disease closely related to excessive weight gain) in the next 10 years. Obesity is increasing in Mexico partly because, in common with many countries, people's eating habits have changed. 'Fast food' is now easily available and is often eaten instead of traditional foods, and this can have damaging effects on health.

CHAPTER 11

Culture and Religion

exico has a very rich culture, reflecting its varied and eventful history, including both ancient Mexican civilizations and Spanish colonization. There are numerous examples of Mayan and Aztec architectural influences, especially in the colours and designs used to decorate buildings. Spanish influence is particularly strong in the architecture of the central and southern regions, where many houses have an interior courtyard and wrought-iron grilles to protect the windows. Under Spanish rule, towns were planned with straight streets leading into a main square (*plaza mayor*).

ART, MUSIC AND FOOD

There is a strong tradition of folk art and crafts, with particular regions specializing in different products, such as silver-working in central Mexico and hammocks from Yucatán. There are many skilled Mexican wood-carvers, and wooden masks have been popular since they were first used in the dances of ancient Mexico and later, in the sixteenth, seventeenth and eighteenth centuries, under Spanish rule. Painting has a long history in Mexico, and some Mexican painters have achieved worldwide fame. Perhaps the most widely known artists were the muralists, including Diego Rivera, who produced some of the greatest revolutionary art of the twentieth century, between the 1920s and the 1950s. The two presidents who came to office after the Mexican Revolution, Alvaro Obregón (1920-1924) and Plutarco Calles (1924-1934), enlisted artists, including Rivera, to produce works that would portray the violence and heroism of the

▼ Mariachi bands used to play at weddings in the nineteenth century. Nowadays they are more often seen playing for tourists in many parts of Mexico.

Revolution. Rivera's huge murals, many of which are displayed in or on public buildings, depict the Mexican struggle for independence.

Like Mexican painting, traditional Mexican music also contains cultural echoes from the past. Fiestas often include live music played on a range of instruments, including the reed flute and conch shell, that originated in ancient Mexico. Meanwhile, stringed instruments, such as violins and guitars, were introduced to Mexico during the Spanish conquest. One of the best-known styles of music played with these stringed instruments is mariachi, which originated in Jalisco State. Mariachi bands can consist of anywhere between four and fifteen members.

Mexican cuisine is very distinctive and is the result of the mixing of cultures of the ancient

▲ Tacos are a traditional type of stuffed tortilla, made from maize or wheat flour.

civilizations, colonial Spain and, more recently, influences from the USA. Corn and two other widely used ingredients, beans and chillies, provide the basic diet for many Mexicans, and have done so since ancient times. There are many regional variations in the types of food and the way they are cooked, but the use of corn (maize) in tortillas is found all over the country.

 Did you know?

Both vanilla and chocolate were first used as flavourings by the ancient Mexican civilizations and were introduced to other countries through trade.

THE FAMILY AND ITS TRADITIONS

Traditionally, the family has been the most important social institution in Mexican society. For many Mexicans, this is still the case today, although social attitudes are changing, particularly among those with the highest levels of income and education. The most significant changes in Mexican family life are those affecting the role of women. During the 1970s and 1980s, economic hardship meant that more women went out to work because their earnings were needed as well as those of the male breadwinner. Since then, more women have become economically independent. Many women now wish to have a more active role in society beyond that of the family unit. The changing role of women can sometimes conflict with 'machismo', the traditional code of behaviour according to which men are expected to be strong, proud and in control. However, an increasing number of men want to be more involved in bringing up their children.

▲ Families celebrate Independence Day together. These children in Mexico City are dressed up for the occasion.

RELIGIOUS BELIEFS AND PRACTICES

Most Mexicans are Catholic, the religion of the Spanish conquistadors. However, they practise a characteristically Mexican form of Catholicism, merging Catholic beliefs with those of the religions of the ancient Mexican civilizations, as in the celebration of the Day of the Dead festival. Another example involves the patron saint of Mexico, the Virgin of Guadalupe. In 1531, an Indian peasant at Tepeyac, near Mexico City, saw a vision of a dark-skinned Virgin Mary who instructed him to build a shrine to her. The Aztec goddess, Tonantzin, had been worshipped at the same site, and many believed the peasant's vision to be the re-apparition of this goddess. Over two million pilgrims visit this shrine on 12 December each year.

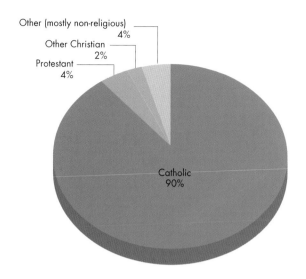

Other (mostly non-religious) 4%
Other Christian 2%
Protestant 4%
Catholic 90%

▲ Major religions

▲ The eighteenth-century cathedral in Chihuahua.

Focus on: The Day of the Dead festival

Every year, on the first two days of November, the people of Mexico remember their dead relations in a festival called the Day of the Dead. The festivities vary from place to place but all combine a sense of fun with a deeper spirituality. The souls of the dead are thought to visit their living relatives over these two days and are welcomed with special decorations, including skeletons and skulls made from papier mâché, chocolate and sugar. Day of the Dead celebrations may also include candle-lit processions to cemeteries. Elements of ancient religious and Christian rituals are included in the festivities, with Aztec beliefs about Mictlantecuhtli, Lord of the Underworld, blending with the Christian celebration of All Saints Day.

▲ People celebrating the Day of the Dead may wear skull masks and clothes with bones painted on them.

CHAPTER 12

Leisure and Tourism

Mexicans are very keen on playing and watching a range of sports, and football is particularly popular. Mexico has hosted the World Cup finals twice, in 1970 and 1986. Another much-loved national sport is wrestling (*lucha libre*). Wrestlers dress in theatrical costumes, wear masks and take on names like *El Santo* ('The Saint') or *El Vampiro* ('The Vampire'). Bull-fighting is also very popular and has been part of Mexican culture for about five hundred years. There are hundreds of bullrings in Mexico, including the largest in the world, in Mexico City, which can seat 50,000.

FAMILY AND HOME ENTERTAINMENT

Much leisure time is spent with family members – either cooking and eating at home or going out together. Local celebrations also provide family entertainment, including fireworks, music and dancing. Dance is a popular leisure activity, and young children are

▼ *Charrería* is the Mexican art of horsemanship. This involves horse-riders demonstrating their skills on horseback in an arena similar to a bullring, accompanied by mariachi music.

taught social dances, such as 'merengue' and 'salsa', at family fiestas. There are numerous festivals throughout the year and each one is celebrated in a different way, with special foods and events. Some of these festivals are public holidays, marking significant social and historical events such as *Cinco de Mayo* (which commemorates a Mexican victory over France in 1862). Others are religious, such as Semana Santa (Easter Week).

Many Mexicans spend much of their leisure time watching television, and some of the most popular programmes are the many soap operas (*telenovelas*). The most successful of these can draw audiences of 25 million. They are made in Mexico, specifically for Mexican audiences, by the two main national broadcasters, Televisa and TV Azteca. *Telenovela* actors are celebrities in Mexican society and are often featured in magazines and newspaper gossip columns. As well as magazines and newspapers, people also enjoy reading *historieta* – pocket-sized comic books written for an adult audience.

▲ Tourism not only benefits hotel workers and tour guides. The increased money in the local economy can also encourage the expansion of the informal economy, such as this shoeshiner in Guadalajara.

THE IMPACT OF TOURISM

Tourism is a major generator of foreign earnings for Mexico, and has become the largest single source of employment in the country, offering many jobs in tourist facilities, such as hotels and restaurants, and providing activities like scuba diving and golf. There are also many more jobs in the informal sector, like selling hand-made souvenirs at roadside stalls and cleaning shoes on city streets. There are about 20 million tourists a year, mostly from the USA, but Mexico's appeal is widening and the country is now the eighth most popular holiday destination in the world. Tourist developments are very varied. For example, there are luxurious, purpose-built resorts, such as Cancún, where accommodation, restaurants, shops and leisure activities are all provided in one place, and there are also 'ecotourism' trips and facilities that cater for different tastes and budgets.

▲ The Acapulco divers are one of Mexico's most famous tourist attractions. Young men climb to the top of a cliff and dive into a narrow sea channel below. Timing is crucial, as the water is only deep enough when a wave swells through the channel.

Tourists come to Mexico for many reasons. Sandy beaches and warm seas, particularly along the Yucatán coast, appeal to those who want a beach holiday, while archaeological discoveries, such as those found at the Mayan site of Chichén Itzá, attract those with an interest in history and different cultures. Local customs and crafts (including markets, dress, folk art and jewellery-making) are also of interest to some tourists.

Mexico's varied physical environments, with their wide range of animal and plant species, attract ecotourists. For instance, it is possible to go into the mountainous interior of Baja California to spot great horned sheep, or to visit the Pacific island of San Benito – a refuge for elephant seals. Recently, there has been increasing interest in organized trips into wilderness areas, including hiking tours into the remote south-west of Tabasco.

However, there are risks attached to Mexico's dependence on tourism for jobs and foreign revenue. Firstly, the tourist trade is vulnerable to disruption from natural hazards. For example, Hurricane Pauline seriously damaged the popular tourist resort of Acapulco in 1997. Even though the government and city authorities made sure that tourist areas were cleaned up within a few weeks, six months later tourist

Tourism data

- Tourist arrivals, millions: 19.667
- Earnings from tourism in US$: 8,858,000,000
- Tourism as % foreign earnings: 5
- Tourist departures, millions: 11.948
- Expenditure on tourism in US$: 6,060,000,000

Source: World Bank

figures were down by 15 per cent – perhaps because potential visitors did not know about the speedy clear-up or were nervous about the risk of another hurricane. Other factors affecting tourist numbers include changes in the currency exchange rate, and fear of terrorism. For instance, numbers of US tourists fell significantly for a couple of years after the 9/11 attacks.

Focus on: Hot springs and spa resorts

Because of Mexico's numerous volcanoes, there are many places where hot mineral springs bubble up from underground. These provide mineral and spa baths, believed by many to help tackle stress and health problems such as skin conditions, and there is evidence that wealthy Aztecs enjoyed them in ancient times. Many of these spa facilities are quite simple – just a swimming pool filled with warm, murky brown mineral water – and are mostly used at weekends by Mexican families. However, there are also several spa resorts catering for tourists, with luxury hotels.

▼ Some natural spas in Mexico have been developed into major leisure attractions, such as here in Puebla.

CHAPTER 13

Environment and Conservation

Air pollution is a huge problem in industrial areas where companies have not been subject to emission controls and in large urban settlements with high levels of vehicle emissions. Ciudad Juárez, an industrial town on the Mexican-US border, is one of the worst-affected places. More than a million trucks pass through the town every year, leaving high levels of suspended particles in the air. This type of pollution causes serious health problems (including asthma and respiratory disease), particularly among children.

The government has now brought in measures to tackle air pollution and these include tax incentives to encourage industries to buy pollution control equipment. All petrol sold by the national oil company, PEMEX, has been lead-free since 1998. And, in 2000, Mexico signed the Kyoto Protocol, an international treaty that aims to reduce greenhouse gas emissions. By 2004, Mexico had made some progress in slowing down the rate of increase in emissions, although it had not yet been able to significantly reduce the air pollution problem. However, Mexico's greenhouse gas emissions are still well below those of highly industrialized countries and are the equivalent of those of the USA 50 years ago.

▼ Smog, caused by air pollution, hangs over Mexico City. The government is trying to reduce emissions from vehicles and industry.

Environmental and conservation data

📁 Forested area as % total land area: 29

📁 Protected area as % total land area: 5

📁 Number of protected areas: 150

SPECIES DIVERSITY

Category	Known species (1992-2002)	Threatened species (2002)
Mammals	491	70
Breeding birds	440	39
Reptiles	837	18
Amphibians	358	4
Fish	674	95
Plants	26,071	221

Source: World Resources Institute

PROBLEMS WITH WATER

Water pollution is widespread in urban and industrial areas, often due to the discharge of waste. Only 25 per cent of urban waste water is treated (cleaned of pollutants), and industrial waste water is largely left untreated. There are also problems with coastal waters. The Gulf of Mexico is affected by petroleum spills and also by untreated sewage, industrial waste, pesticides and fertilizers being washed into it. The government is committed to building more treatment plants and to raising awareness of the pollution problems but it will take time for its water treatment measures to take effect. The aim is for 41 per cent of urban waste water and 15 per cent of industrial waste water to be treated by 2006. In the longer term, the goal is 60 per cent overall waste water treatment by 2025.

Another problem is the over-exploitation of water supplies. As agriculture has become more intensive, farmers have needed to use more irrigation, and groundwater and rivers have become depleted, especially in the drier northern areas.

Overuse of groundwater has also caused problems in Mexico City. The city is sited on an aquifer (a type of underground lake), from which water has been pumped to meet the rising demands of the huge population. As water has been removed, the sediments of the aquifer have become compressed, and so the city has sunk about 10 m (33 feet) over the past century. In both the north and Mexico City, attempts are now being made to use and transport water more efficiently in order to reduce demand.

 Did you know?

The Rio Bravo/Rio Grande did not reach the sea in February 2001 because so much water had been used, mainly for irrigation, in the area of its drainage basin.

▲ Irrigation is used to grow over half of Mexico's agricultural produce, especially export crops such as the pecan nuts produced by these trees.

BIODIVERSITY: THREATS AND PROTECTION

Mexico is classed as a megadiverse country, with 12 per cent of the world's total biodiversity (animal and plant species). It also has one of the highest rates of deforestation in the world. About 770,000 hectares (1,902,643 acres) of forest are cleared every year in order to rear livestock and cultivate crops. Although the government has pledged to reduce deforestation by 75 per cent between 2001 and 2025, protected areas only made up 5 per cent of the country's territory in 2003. Outside protected areas, it is far harder to prevent people from felling trees and destroying ecosystems. Positive national government initiatives have included the establishment of the National Commission for the Knowledge and

Use of Biodiversity in 1992. Mexico is also party to over 100 international environmental agreements. Local and national projects have been set up under these agreements, including a sanctuary for grey whales, protected under the

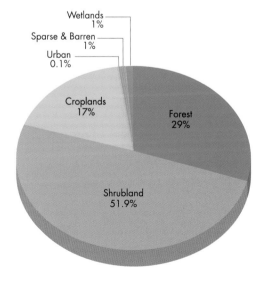

▲ Habitat type as percentage of total area

World Heritage Convention. Mexico also participates in the Green Globe 21, an international sustainable tourism certificate, set up following the Rio Earth Summit in 1992 when many countries met to discuss how to tackle global environmental problems. To gain the certificate, tourist companies or resorts have to put principles of sustainability, such as water and energy conservation, into practice. Few have been fully certificated but many tourist enterprises are working towards it. In addition, with eco-tourism depending on environmental attractions, there is a strong commercial incentive to protect habitats as well as an increased awareness of their global significance. For example, whale-watching trips off the coast of Baja California attract many tourists and also help to ensure that the whales are protected.

THE GOAL OF SUSTAINABILITY

Sustainable development has become an explicit goal in Mexico's National Development Plan, and this means that government funding is available for some environmental protection initiatives. World Bank loans have also been used to help Mexico balance economic development with sustainability, through such initiatives as the Renewable Energy Programme. This programme promotes the development of wind and solar energy, for which Mexico has great potential capacity.

▲ Monarch butterflies at the Monarch Butterfly Sanctuary in Michoacan. Every year, millions of monarchs make the 4,828 km (3,000 mile) round trip between their winter roosts, in the mountains of central Mexico, and their summer haunts in the USA.

Focus on: Recyling through 'scavenging'

Recycling of waste is another important aspect of sustainability. Currently, people known as 'scavengers' work on urban landfills, making a living from selling recyclable materials and also helping to improve Mexico's levels of sustainability. Working within the unhealthy conditions of landfill sites means that these people have a higher incidence of disease and a shorter life expectancy. However, if the municipal authorities were to control and mechanize the retrieving of recyclable material, the 'scavengers' would almost certainly lose their livelihoods. For these reasons, the 'scavengers' are opposed to any municipal regulation of recycling waste.

CHAPTER 14

Future Challenges

In the twenty-first century, Mexico faces a number of challenges. Economic development since the Second World War has given many people a better quality of life but there is concern that the pace of development is not keeping up with population growth. Over 53 million people have poor access to adequate basic services (clean water, sanitation and electricity), and with approximately 1.5 million new citizens every year this situation is likely to worsen. Mexico has one of the biggest gaps between rich and poor sectors of society in the world. Economic improvements are unequally distributed, mainly benefiting the north and Mexico City, while the south remains poor. There is also great poverty in the urban slums and shanty towns of Mexico's cities and towns.

SUSTAINABLE DEVELOPMENT?

Finding a balance between economic development and the protection of the environment is another challenge, which has become the focus of recent initiatives funded by the World Bank. The Mexican government has also made sustainable development one of its highest priorities. Of the many environmental issues to be tackled, groundwater depletion and water shortage are causing particular concern. Demand for water is increasing because of population growth and economic development, especially the spread of more commercial forms

▼ Flamingos taking flight in Celestun Nature Reserve. The government has set up a number of such reserves in order to preserve Mexico's wildlife.

of agriculture, which require a lot of irrigation. In many areas, farmers are struggling with water shortages, and in the northern border area water scarcity is also a source of friction between the USA and Mexico.

CROSS-BORDER ISSUES

Illegal migration to the USA has a negative effect on Mexican settlements, which lose many young, economically active people. Both countries are adopting strategies to deal with this issue. For Mexico, these strategies include improving living conditions and increasing job opportunities so that people do not have to migrate to better themselves.

Drug trafficking is another continuing cross-border issue. Heroin and cannabis originate from Mexican sources, and cocaine is smuggled through Mexico from further south. The Mexican government does have drug crop eradication schemes in place and these are seen as vital in tackling the problem.

MEXICAN NATIONAL IDENTITY

There is concern among some Mexicans that their culture, with all its richness and diversity, will be lost or 'watered down' in the face of increasing contact with ideas and practices from the USA. It is certainly true that there are more US 'fast-food' outlets in Mexico and more Hollywood movies being shown than there used to be. However, there is still a clear sense of national identity, underpinned by the concept of

Mexicanidad (Mexican-ness). Fundamental to this sense of identity are the influences of the ancient civilizations, awareness of European invasion and conquest, and the legacy of the struggles of the Mexican Revolution.

▼ Pancho Villa, one of the leaders of the Mexican Revolution, led his army from northern Mexico to fight against the dictatorship of Porfirio Diaz. He was assassinated in 1923, and about 30,000 people attended his funeral.

Timeline

200 BC-AD 1200 Development of great urban civilizations, e.g. Maya, Zapotecs.

1325 Aztecs settle in central Mexico.

1519 Hernán Cortés leads Spanish troops to Mexico in search of gold and silver.

1521-1821 Mexico is renamed New Spain, and becomes a colony of Spain for three centuries.

1821 Mexico wins independence.

1824 Democratic federal republic of Mexico is established.

1876 General Porfirio Diaz seizes power and rules as a dictator for 35 years.

1910-1917 Mexican Revolution to overthrow dictatorship and establish rights of all citizens.

1917 Present-day Mexican Constitution drawn up.

1942 Mexico declares war on Japan and Germany in the Second World War.

1945 Mexico joins the United Nations.

1950 Television introduced in Mexico.

1954 Mexican women gain right to vote.

1968 Mexico hosts the Olympic Games. Government troops open fire on student demonstration, killing hundreds.

1969 Subway opens in Mexico City.

1976 Mexico hosts the finals of the football World Cup for the first time. The second time is in 1986.

1982 Oil prices drop, leading to Mexico suffering a huge debt crisis and being unable to repay foreign loans.

1985 Mexico City is hit by earthquake measuring 8.1 on Richter scale. Over 20,000 are killed.

1994 Mexico joins the USA and Canada in the North American Free Trade Agreement (NAFTA).

Uprising of Indians in the Chiapas region of Mexico.

1998 Closure of the world's biggest silver mine at Real de Angeles.

2000 Vicente Fox, of the National Action Party, is elected as President of Mexico, ending 70 years of domination by the Institutional Revolutionary Party.

Volcano Popocatépetl, near Mexico City, erupts for the first time since the 1920s.

2001 The Zapatista National Liberation Army, representing the Indians in Chiapas region, stage a two-week march to Mexico City calling for Congress to approve a bill on Indian rights.

Glossary

Altitude The height of the land above sea level, sometimes known as elevation.

Aquifer An underground source of water where rainwater has seeped into a layer of porous rock.

Biodiversity Variety of forms of life.

Constitution A document that sets out the rights and responsibilities of a government and its citizens.

Coup An event that occurs when a group of people suddenly get together to try to overthrow those in power. A coup is often led by military personnel.

Deputy An elected representative in the Chamber of Deputies of the federal government, who debates and helps decide whether or not to pass laws.

Dictatorship A form of government in which the ruler (or dictator) has complete power.

Federal republic A form of government with two layers. The Mexican Republic consists of the federal government at national level and the governments of 31 states and the federal district of Mexico City.

Greenhouse gases Gases in the Earth's atmosphere (e.g. carbon dioxide, methane and nitrous oxides) that trap the heat from the sun, keeping it in the atmosphere.

Gross Domestic Product (GDP) Total value of goods and services produced within the borders of a country.

Gross National Income (GNI) Total value of a country's income from goods and services produced by its residents both within the country and elsewhere in the world. For instance, the profits of a US-owned factory in Mexico will be counted as part of the USA's GNI.

Illiterate Unable to read or write.

Independence (Of a country) The right to control its own affairs.

Indigenous people The original or native population who first lived in an area or country.

Infrastructure Networks that allow communication and/or help people and the economy to function, e.g. roads, railways, electricity and telephone lines.

Literacy The ability to read and write.

Maquiladora A factory, usually located near the Mexican-US border, where goods, mainly intended for sale in the USA, are produced relatively cheaply.

Mariachi music Traditional Mexican music originating in the eighteenth century and played by a small band, usually including a guitarist, violinist and trumpet player.

National Congress The elected body of government, made up of the Senate and the Chamber of Deputies, in which the laws of the nation are passed.

Rapid transit system A public transport system (e.g. bus or rail) designed to carry large numbers of people as quickly as possible in large congested urban areas.

Reservoir Water stored for use by humans.

'Scavenger' A person who makes his or her living by finding items and materials, dumped on refuse tips, that can be recycled.

Seismic activity Earthquakes and volcanic eruptions.

Senator An elected member of the Senate (which is part of the federal government), who helps decide on the laws of the country.

Shanty town A collection of temporary dwellings made of scrap materials and built on the edges of cities in less developed countries by people with little or no income.

Sisal Fibre produced from the leaves of a plant and used to make rope.

Sustainable development Economic development that can be continued without damaging the environment.

Tectonic area Region affected by earthquakes and volcanoes triggered by movements of large sections of the Earth's crust, known as tectonic plates.

Tsunami A very large ocean wave caused by an earthquake or volcanic eruption beneath the sea.

Waste water treatment Removal of pollutants and harmful substances from water that has been used in households or by industries.

Further Information

BOOKS TO READ

Horrible Histories: The Angry Aztecs
Terry Deary
(Scholastic Hippo, 2004)

Countries of the World: Mexico
Edward Parker
(Evans Brothers, 2004)

Letters from Around the World: Mexico
P. Cunningham
(Cherry Tree Books, 2004)

The Changing Face of Mexico
Edward Parker
(Hodder Wayland, 2004)

World Art and Craft: Mexican Art and Craft
E. Lewis
(Heinemann, 2003)

In Focus: Mexico – A Guide to the People, Politics and Culture
J. Ross
(Latin American Bureau/ Interlink Books, 2003)

USEFUL WEBSITES

www.elbalero.gob.mx/kids/
A site run by the Presidency of Mexico and providing information about aspects of the country, such as its history and biodiversity.

www.mexconnect.com/
An electronic magazine with many articles about Mexico. Has a good search capability.

www.inside-mexico.com/
A magazine-style site with articles and a newsletter about various aspects of Mexico.

www.settlement.org/cp/english/mexico/
A Canadian government website giving general information about many aspects of life in Mexico.

www.monarchwatch.org
Gives information about the great migrations of monarch butterflies between Mexico and the USA. Includes section on how young people can get involved in tagging butterflies.

www.unicef.org/infobycountry/mexico_statistics.htm
UNICEF website with country profile and population statistics.

www.earthtrends.org/
Statistics for selected countries including Mexico.

www.state.gov/background_notes/mexico
US government site providing facts and figures about Mexico.

www.odci.gov/cia/publications/factbook/geos/mx
Offers the CIA facts and figures on Mexico.

www.eia.doe.gov/emeu/cabs/mexico.html
Contains two detailed country profiles of Mexico, provided by the US Department of Energy.

Index

Page numbers in **bold** indicate pictures.

About the Author

Celia Tidmarsh is a geography PGCE tutor at the Graduate School of Education, University of Bristol. She has taught geography in secondary schools in the UK for 15 years. She has written a number of geography textbooks on various topics for young people, and has also carried out research into children's attitudes to nature and environmental issues.